First World War
and Army of Occupation
War Diary
France, Belgium and Germany

18 DIVISION
Headquarters, Branches and Services
Senior Chaplain (C of E)
1 August 1916 - 30 November 1916

WO95/2023/4

The Naval & Military Press Ltd
www.nmarchive.com
Published in association with The National Archives

Published by

The Naval & Military Press Ltd

Unit 10 Ridgewood Industrial Park,

Uckfield, East Sussex,

TN22 5QE England

Tel: +44 (0) 1825 749494

www.naval-military-press.com

www.nmarchive.com

This diary has been reprinted in facsimile from the original. Any imperfections are inevitably reproduced and the quality may fall short of modern type and cartographic standards.

© Crown Copyright
Images reproduced by permission of The National Archives, London, England, 2015.

Contents

Document type	Place/Title	Date From	Date To
Heading	WO95/2023/4		
Heading	18th Division Senr. Chaplain Aug-Nov 1916		
Heading	Vol 1 Senior Chaplain Church of England 18th Division Aug 16 Nov 1916		
War Diary	Ranescure	01/08/1916	01/08/1916
War Diary	Croix Du Bac	02/08/1916	23/08/1916
War Diary	Croix Du Bac total Bailleul	24/08/1916	24/08/1916
War Diary	Bailleul to Roellecourt Via S. Pol.	25/08/1916	25/08/1916
War Diary	Roellecourt	26/08/1916	06/09/1916
War Diary	Roellecourt to Doullens	09/09/1916	09/09/1916
War Diary	Doullens	10/09/1916	10/09/1916
War Diary	Doullens To Acheux	11/09/1916	11/09/1916
War Diary	At-Acheux	12/09/1916	14/09/1916
War Diary	Acheux	14/09/1916	25/09/1916
War Diary	Hedauville	26/09/1916	30/09/1916
Heading	War Diary of the Chaplain's Department. C. of E. 18th Division For The Month Of October 1916 Vol. III		
War Diary	Hedauville	01/10/1916	05/10/1916
War Diary	Bernaville	06/10/1916	15/10/1916
War Diary	Albert	16/10/1916	29/10/1916
Heading	War Diary of the Senior Chaplain C. of E. 18th Division for the month of November 1916 Volume IV		
War Diary	Albert	01/11/1916	22/11/1916
War Diary	Buigny	23/11/1916	23/11/1916
War Diary	St Maclou	25/11/1916	30/11/1916

WP(C) 2095/2023 (4)

18TH DIVISION

SENR. CHAPLAIN
AUG - NOV 1916

Vol 1

Senior Chaplain

Church of England

18th Division

Aug '16 - Nov 1916

Army Form C. 2118

S.C.F. 18th Division

WAR DIARY or INTELLIGENCE SUMMARY

(Erase heading not required.)

Place	Date 1916	Hour	Summary of Events and Information	Remarks and references to Appendices
Rawcourt	August 1		Nothing to report.	
Croix du Bac	2		Moved from Rawcourt to Croix du Bac with D.H.Q.	
" "	3		Received from A.C.G. II nd Army suggested form of Prayer & letter from D.C.G. suggesting Special Services for following Sunday in view of fact that Aug 4th is 2nd Anniversary of England's declaration of War with Germany. This copy of form of Prayer by Courtesy of "A" Branch, D.H.Q. copies for S.C.F. in sufficient numbers to be forwarded at once to all Divisional Chaplains. With above some copies of printed letter from the D.C.G. addressed to all ranks on the same subject, one of which was forwarded to all Chaplains.	
" "	4		2nd Anniversary of Declaration of War by England against Germany. Visited C.R.E. unit No. 1 at Eclaires to ascertain exact location of Burial Ground in Area now held by Division. Information to A. Branch forwarded. G.A.W.	3

Army Form C. 2118

WAR DIARY or INTELLIGENCE SUMMARY

S.C.F. 18th Division 9/E

Place	Date	Hour	Summary of Events and Information	Remarks and references to Appendices
Colk du Bac	1916 August 5th		S.C.F. Rev. G.A. WESTON left for England on 14 days local leave on having resigned Contract for another year's service. Rev. R.P. SHINER took over duties of S.C.F. for above period coming from No. 2 Section, D.A.C. to S.C.F. billeted D.A.Q. H&S	4
	6th		Sunday. Reference made by all Chaplains at services of to-day to occasion of 2nd Anniversary of Declaration of War. A.C.G's letter on the subject also special prayers suggested by D.C.G. used. More copies of D.C.G's letter were received & distributed to some of all ranks though a sufficient number were not received for distribution to all.	

Army Form C. 2118

WAR DIARY
or
INTELLIGENCE SUMMARY

S.C.F. (C of E) 18th Division

(Erase heading not required.)

Instructions regarding War Diaries and Intelligence Summaries are contained in F. S. Regs., Part II. and the Staff Manual respectively. Title Pages will be prepared in manuscript.

Place	Date	Hour	Summary of Events and Information	Remarks and references to Appendices
Croix du Bac	1916 August 7th		Nothing to report.	
"	8th		" " "	
"	9th		Chaplain V.C. BODDINGTON. Capt. C of E. 8th batt. left England Aug 8th arrived from St Omer to join Division vice Rev. R.P. SHINER whose contract expires July 25th.	
"	10th		Chaplain V.C. BODDINGTON C/E attached to 7th Buffs, 55th Inf. Brigade vice Rev J.S. SHARP. C/E this day transferred to No 2 Section D.A.C. (attached) & allotted to H.Q.R.A. vice Rev. R.P. SHINER acting S.C.F. & about to return to England.	
"	11th		Nothing to report.	
"	12th		Chaplain D. RANDELL. C/E attached 10th Essex Regt. reported sick & has been sent to Divisional Rest for Officers - hosp. 10 days	5

1875 Wt. W503/826 1,000,000 4/15 J.B.C. & A. A.D.S.S./Forms/C. 2118.

WAR DIARY or INTELLIGENCE SUMMARY

Army Form C. 2118

S.C.F. C/E
18th Division

Place	Date	Hour	Summary of Events and Information	Remarks and references to Appendices
Croix du Bac	1916 July 13		Nothing to report.	G.A.C.
"	14		"	G.A.C.
"	15		"	G.A.C.
"	16		Rev. D. Rowdell. C.F. (1st Essex, 53rd Inf. Bde) evacuated from 1st Australian C.C.S. (Estaires) to Base with Pyrexia. Test for Enteric, of which he had been suspected, has proved negative.	G.A.C.
				G.A.C.
	17		Nothing to report	G.A.C.
	18		"	G.A.C.
	19		Rev. G.A. WESTON. Sc.F. C/E Div returned from leave having landed at Boulogne day previously. Rev. R.P. SHINER left Division to proceed to England his contract having expired on July 25 & not renewed. His departure duly reported to D.A.D.Q. of not Army. A.C.G. 4th Army. G.A.C.	6

Army Form C. 2118

WAR DIARY
or
INTELLIGENCE SUMMARY

C.7. of 8th Division

(Erase heading not required.)

Place	Date	Hour	Summary of Events and Information	Remarks and references to Appendices
Croix du Bac	1916 April 20		Services as practicable through Division excepting for 2 Battalions in trenches. Introduced subject of National Mission & Repentance & Hope in Repose addresses at #HQ.	G.A.C.
"	21		Heard from Rev. D. RANDELL at No 14 Stationary Hospital Base — that further tests for Typhoid were negative: that he hopes to avoid being invalided to England & to rejoin his Brigade. Advised him to apply for sick leave.	G.A.C. G.A.C. G.A.C.
"	22		" " Nothing to report.	G.A.C.
"	23		" " " "	G.A.C.
Croix du Bac / Bailleul	24		Moved Division. D.H.Q. left Croix du Bac in morning for Bailleul — billet there for night. Prepared to return next day.	G.A.C.

7

WAR DIARY
INTELLIGENCE SUMMARY

S. & E. 8th Division

Place	Date	Hour	Summary of Events and Information	Remarks and references to Appendices
Bailleul to Roellecourt via St. Pol.	1916 August 25	10.28 am	Entrained with D.H.Q. at Bailleul for St. Pol.	
		2.0 pm	Arrived at St. Pol – Detrained & proceeded to Roellecourt.	
		4.0 "		
		6.0 "	Sent circular to all C of E chaplains (except Rev J.S. SHARP attached 18 A.C. who remained behind with R.A. of Div.) informing them of distribution of troops in new area & suggesting plan of co-operation to provide Services for all troops in new area. GLW.	
Roellecourt	26		Riding over part of new area to arrange re Sunday Services. GLW	
"	27		Few Services this Sunday in Inf Brigades as Training was going on as on Week days. GLW	

WAR DIARY

Army Form C. 2118

S.C.F. c/E 18th Division

Place	Date 1916 Aug.	Hour	Summary of Events and Information	Remarks and references to Appendices
Roellecourt	28		Nothing to report.	
"	29		Received wire from O.C. No. 14 Stationary Hospital that Rev. D. RANDELL had been granted 21 days sick leave. Reported same to 53rd Inf. Bde, 10th Essex Reg., D.A.Q. & IIIrd Army, G.O.C.	
"	30	6.0 PM	8th Royal Sussex Powers Reg[t]. left Auxi-ouegt to proceed by stages to Doullens. Rev. R.D. CANADINE left with them being attached to Reg[t]. G.O.C.	

9

WAR DIARY or INTELLIGENCE SUMMARY

Army Form C. 2118

S.C.F. of 18 Division

Place	Date	Hour	Summary of Events and Information	Remarks and references to Appendices
Roellecourt	August 31	2.30	Chaplains' Meeting. Present S.C.F., Revs C.H. WELLER & E.A. BENNET (54th Brigade) Revs G.T. STOPFORD & V.C. BODDINGTON 55th Brigade & Rev C.T. PARKINSON 53rd Bde. Proceedings commenced with Devotional Meeting in Mairie above Village School, Roellecourt – Rev. G.A. WESTON. S.C.F. gave short address on National Mission. Penitence & Hope & its bearings on Chaplains' work & prayers & its presentation to the Army out here in France – Summarising the Pamphlets so far published by National Mission & preparing for the Service of Intercession which followed. Other business was then proceeded with – (Rev) Amendments to G.R.O.s re burials & information of deceased were noted & to all chaplains of Division that Devotional Meetings should be repeated.	G.J.S.F. Woolnow 18 Division

Army Form C. 2118

WAR DIARY
or
INTELLIGENCE SUMMARY
(Erase heading not required.)

C.R.E. of 18th Division Vol II

Place	Date	Hour	Summary of Events and Information	Remarks and references to Appendices
ROELLECOURT	1916 Sept 3rd		Sunday. Services held throughout most of Division though somewhat interfered with owing to necessity of continuance of training. e.g. 53rd Inf Bde training all day. Fine weather in morning allowed of open air Church Parades.	
"	5th		Move of Division arranged for to-day postponed till further orders. Received copy of wire A.3rd Army/noting P.G. G.H.Q. 2nd Echelon Chaplain F.G.ILLETT/late 6-54th Bde/vice Rev J.K. PAGET who is to proceed to 2 I.C.C.S. for duty. Rode over to visit 55th Brigade Chaplains at MONCHY BRETON. Learnt from Rev. G. F. STOPFORD that Rev. V.C. BODDINGTON had had considerable numbers of communicants from 7th BUFFS & 7th R.W. KENTS last Sunday. /that he was finding demand for Pocket Testaments. Accordingly do issued a further stock of Active Service Testaments from (continued next page)	11

HEAD QUARTERS 9 OCT. 1916 18TH DIVISION

Army Form C. 2118

A.C.7. C of E
WAR DIARY
or
INTELLIGENCE SUMMARY
18th Division
(Erase heading not required.)

Place	Date Hour	Summary of Events and Information	Remarks and references to Appendices
ROELLECOURT.	September 6th 1916 (Cont)	Complete C of E Mission, 15 Straws W.C. (to be used from Chaplain's Fund 18th Div.) for use of Chaplains in distribution. Also saw Rev. T. HAYWARD, U.B. recently attached 7th Queen's vice Chaplain BELLEW transferred Rouen G.A.C.	
ROELLECOURT. to DOULLENS.	9. —	Whole Division moved from training area East of St Pol. — H.Q. of Div. to DOULLENS. Brigades by stages. G.A.C.	
DOULLENS.	10. —	Sunday. No services owing to travelling — except for D.H.Q. at DOULLENS. G.A.C.	

12

Army Form C. 2118

S.C.7. 18 Division
INTELLIGENCE SUMMARY
(Erase heading not required.)

Place	Date	Hour	Summary of Events and Information	Remarks and references to Appendices
DOULLENS to ACHEUX	1916 Sept 11th		D.H.Q. moves from DOULLENS to ACHEUX - Brigades in area West & S.W. of ACHEUX. (LEALVILLERS, ARQUEVES, RAINCHEVAL, PUCHEVILLERS) Units reported to S.C.7. O/E 2nd Corps.	
ACHEUX	12th		Visited reports to S.C.7 O/E 2nd Corps at SENLIS.	
	14th		Held Chaplains' Meeting - beginning with Celebration of Holy Communion at 10.15 A.M. S.C.7. O/E. 49th Division. Rev. M. W. SHEWELL (Maj.) kindly came over to meeting from Hedauville to give information as to front area West of Thiepval & disposition of Chaplains in that area. All 18th Div. Chaplains present except Rev. T.S. Sharp absent with 18 Bde. R.A. attached to 1st Canadian Division + Rev. D. RANDELL on sick leave.	13

14

Place	Date	Hour	Summary of Events and Information	Remarks
ACHEUX	September 1916 14	8 PM	Received Secret order, Division to be ready to move at 6 hours notice — all stores & kit surplus to G.1098 to be dumped when notice given.	
"	15		Received news of advance on IV & Reserve Army fronts including capture of FLERS and MARTINPUICH.	
"	17		Sunday: 55th Brigade — Church Parade at PUCHEVILLERS for whole Brigade, G.O.C. & Brigade Staff being present, Brigade Chaplain & T.C. BODDINGTON conducting Service. GF STOPFORD Some Services in 53rd Brigade, in spite of movement of Brigade to ACHEUX and BOUZINCOURT.	

Army Form C. 2118

Instructions regarding War Diaries and Intelligence Summaries are contained in F. S. Regs., Part II. and the Staff Manual respectively. Title Pages will be prepared in manuscript.

S.C.T. 8th Division
C. of E.

WAR DIARY
or
INTELLIGENCE SUMMARY

(Erase heading not required.)

15

Place	Date / Hour	Summary of Events and Information	Remarks and references to Appendices
ACHEUX	21	Held Chaplains' Meeting commencing with Celebration of Holy Communion at 10.15 AM.	
"	22	Rev. D. RANDELL rejoined his unit, 10th Essex Reg:t 55th Brigade after 3 weeks sick leave in England. (He arrived in France before midnight Sept 20.)	
"	24	Sunday. Services held so far as movements of various units permitted.	
"	25.	relief of Hq 7th Division whose D.H.Q. were at Hedauville. Divisional Head Quarters moved to Hedauville-relieves Hq 7th Division — with exception of C. Mess including S.C.F. C.J.E. remaining at ACHEUX.	

Army Form C. 2118

S.C.F. C. of E. **WAR DIARY** or
18th Div. **INTELLIGENCE SUMMARY**
(Erase heading not required.)

Place	Date Hour	Summary of Events and Information	Remarks and references to Appendices
ACHEUX	September 25	C. of E. Chaplains V.C. BODDINGTON & G.F. STOPFORD temporarily detached from their Regiments to 55th Brigade & attached to 55th Field Ambulance, Main Dressing Station, Clairfaye Fm CLAIRFAY FARM in readiness for skelter Battle. R.D. CANADINE. C. of E. (2nd Divisional Chaplain) similar detached from 8th Royal Sussex Pioneers & attached to 54th Field Ambulance M.D.S. at VARENNES. Chaplains (C. of E.) of 54th & 53rd Brigades notified that they are to be responsible for all work East of Heading HEDAUVILLE including attention to A.D.S's at BLACK HORSE BRIDGE Map 57.D. S.E. W.11.b.5.1. & Wood Post. AVELUY POST. W.11.b.5.1. & Wood Post. R.A.P. X.1.C.6.4. Map 57.D. S.E. W.6.a.11. also	16

Army Form C. 2118

WAR DIARY
or
INTELLIGENCE SUMMARY

S.C.F. C.of.E. 18th Div.

(Erase heading not required.)

Place	Date	Hour	Summary of Events and Information	Remarks and references to Appendices
HEDAUVILLE	September 26 1916	6 A.M.	C. Mess of S.H.Q. including S.C.F. C of E. moved from ACHEUX to HEDAUVILLE.	
		12.35 PM.	Attack by 53rd & 54th Brigades of the Division which resulted in capture of TH THIEPVAL commenced. S.C.F. after arrival at HEDAUVILLE proceeded to Advanced Dressing Stations at Aveluy Post & BLACK HORSE BRIDGE. Rev. C. H. WELLER was with & working in connection M.O. 12th Middlesex Regt, Rev. E A BENNET similarly with M.O. 6th Northants also keeping touch with A.D.S. of 56th Field Ambulance at BLACK HORSE BRIDGE. Rev. D. RANDELL similarly with M.O. of 10th Essex Regt. Rev. C.T. PARKINSON kept touch with 6th Ryl. Berks, working chiefly at AVELUY POST and WOOD POST (X.I.C.3.S.) Advanced Dressing Stations.	

17

Army Form C. 2118

WAR DIARY
or
INTELLIGENCE SUMMARY

S.C.F. C of E
8th Division

18

Place	Date	Hour	Summary of Events and Information	Remarks and references to Appendices
HEDAUVILLE	September 26		The 2 Chaplains, Rev. C.F. STOPFORD and Rev. V.C. BODDINGTON at CLAIRFAYE FARM. Main Dressing Station working for days from commencement of battle in relief day & night, took charge of arrangements for giving Refreshments (Tea, Cocoa food &c) to walking wounded, besides giving individual attention to spiritual & other temporal needs of the wounded, taking burials at VARENNES Cemetery, & generally assisting in any way open to them. Rev. R.D. CANADINE assisting all this day & night with stretcher cases at 54th Field Ambulance at VARENNES. Both above Dressing Stations visited by S.C.F. after his visits to Advanced Dressing Stations. Rev. C.H. WELLER (attached 1/7th MIDDLESEX) received slight wound from Shrapnel in arm but remained on duty at THIEPVAL.	

Army Form C. 2118

S.C.F. C. of E. WAR DIARY or 18th Division INTELLIGENCE SUMMARY

19

Place	Date	Hour	Summary of Events and Information	Remarks and references to Appendices
HEDAUVILLE	Sept 1916 27		Battle conditions still prevailing. Some burying on battlefield done by forward chaplains & much work at Dressing Stations. Rev. C.H. WELLER (wounded yesterday) evacuated in late evening from CLAIRFAYE M.D.S. with G.S.W. arm. Slight. IVth Army with application for relection of this Chaplain for the Division if possible.	
"	28/9		55th Brigade having relieved 53rd & 54th Brigades in the line, Revs G.F. STOPFORD & V.C. BODDINGTON transferred from M.D.S. at CLAIRFAY to be with their Brigade & attend Advanced Dressing Stations	
"	29th		Rev. J.S. SHARP transferred from Artillery (D.A.C) to relieve Rev. V.C. BODDINGTON & be responsible for Chaplains work at CLAIRFAYE M.D.S.	

Army Form C. 2118

WAR DIARY
or
INTELLIGENCE SUMMARY

A.C.E. Coy E
18th Div.

(Erase heading not required.)

Place	Date	Hour	Summary of Events and Information	Remarks and references to Appendices
HEDAUVILLE	Sept 30		Rev. R.D. GLADDING transferred from M.D.S. at VARENNES to rejoin 8th Royal Sussex Pioneers to be in readiness for burials on battlefield — in particular to assist at same in connection with Divisional Salvage officer's work with Royal Sussex Pioneers, clearing dug outs &c of the dead.	

G.U. Wester
S.C.E. Coy E.
18th Division

Sept 30th 1916.

20

Vol III

War Diary

of the

Chaplain's Department.

C. of. E.

18th Division

for the month of October 1916

Vol. III.

Confidential.

G. A. Weston
S.C.F. C of E.
18th Div.

WAR DIARY

Army Form C. 2118

J.C.F. C of E.
18th Div INTELLIGENCE SUMMARY Volume III p.61

22

Place	Date	Hour	Summary of Events and Information	Remarks and references to Appendices
HEDAUVILLE	October 1		Sunday. Services held for 54th Brigade by Rev. E.A. BENNET (6th Northants) & for 53rd Brigade by Rev. D. RANDELL 9 at D.H.Q by S.C.F. - 55th Brigade & 6th Royal Berks (53rd) being in line in & beyond Thiepval no other services possible. Rev. E.A. BENNET temporarily detached from 6th Northants & R.D. CANADINE " " " 8th R. Sussex Pioneers to join Rev. V.C. BODDINGTON & C.T. PARKINSON in being attached to Corps Salvage Party (Cavalry) to take burial services & be responsible for marking of graves during clearing of battlefield. S.C.F. went round trenches & battlefield in company with D.A.A.& Q.M.G. who was bounding out & delimiting areas & parties into which Salvage Party was to be divided.	
	3rd			

Army Form C. 2118

WAR DIARY
or
INTELLIGENCE SUMMARY

S.C.F. C. of E.
18th Div.
Vol III

Place	Date	Hour	Summary of Events and Information	Remarks and references to Appendices
HEDAUVILLE	Oct 13th	continued	Revd F.A. BENNET & V.C. BODDINGTON who had been previously burying on battlefield accompanied party to assist in indicating areas which had been & which remained to be cleared of bodies.	
"	4		Chaplains above mentioned working with Corps dahr. Party completed burial of bodies in the open & the trenches. Revd F.A. BENNET, R.D. CANADINE & Revd V.C. BODDINGTON. C.T. PARKINSON returned to their units: Revd F.A. BENNET, remained at BLACK HORSE BRIDGE to assist as might be required whilst clearance of dug outs should be going on.	
"	5 p.m.		Papers & information relative to Cemeteries, Drawing Stations, Church Huts applied for re handed to S.C.F. C of E 39th Division whoever ? in preparation for move of Division.	23

Army Form C. 2118

Vol III. p.3.

WAR DIARY
or
INTELLIGENCE SUMMARY S.C.F. C of E
18th Division

24

Place	Date Hour	Summary of Events and Information	Remarks and references to Appendices
BERNAVILLE.	October 6th	Division relieved by 39th Division. D.H.Q moved to BERNAVILLE: remainder of Division moving to villages adjacent – 53rd Bde HQ to MEILLARD 54th Bde HQ to RIBEAUCOURT – 55th Bde HQ to FIENVILLERS.	
	8th	Sunday services throughout Division under comparatively favourable circumstances.	
	11th	Recreation Rooms opened for 54th Brigade & for Div. H.Q & Royal Sussex Pioneers by Revs E.A. BENNET & Senior Chaplain respectively. Orders received same day for move forward of Royal Sussex Pioneers & 53rd Brigade Group	

Army Form C. 2118

Vol III p 4.

WAR DIARY
or
INTELLIGENCE SUMMARY

S.C.F. C of E 18th Division

25

Place	Date	Hour	Summary of Events and Information	Remarks and references to Appendices
BERNAVILLE	1916 Oct 12th	10 AM	Chaplains' Meeting held at S.C.F.'s (C of E) quarters	
BERNAVILLE			Rev. R.D. CANADINE transferred from 8th Rgl. Sussex Pioneers to 54th Field Ambulance, owing to former moving to line, & latter being in 54th Brigade area, a chaplain being needed for Sunday Services in place of Rev. C.H. WELLER wounded. Chaplains D. RANDELL & C.T. PARKINSON now on leave.	
"	15th		Sunday. 55th & 54th Brigade groups moving forward to forward area with their Brigade 53rd forward area (Reserve Army T.J.) A few Services held in Division as circumstances allowed.	

WAR DIARY

Army Form C. 2118

Vol III p 5
S.C.F, C of E INTELLIGENCE SUMMARY
18th Div.

Place	Date	Hour	Summary of Events and Information	Remarks and references to Appendices
ALBERT	1916 Oct 16th		2nd Echelon D.H.Q. (with S.C.) moved from BERNAVILLE & rejoined 1st Echelon which had previously gone to ALBERT.	
	17th		Chaplains of 55th Brigade arrived with their Brigade in ALBERT. Chaplain E.A. Bennet 54th " " " BOUZINCOURT. Chaplains of 53rd " " " " in touch with their Brigade in the right of line support West + NW of COURCELETTE. Orders received from A.C.G. IV Army notifying appointment of Rev. N.S. TALBOT. MC as A.C.G. Reserve Army as from Thursday Oct 19th — all correspondence & returns to be addressed to him instead of A.C.G. IV Army from that date.	26

Army Form C. 2118

Vol VIII p 6

WAR DIARY
or
INTELLIGENCE SUMMARY
(Erase heading not required.)

S.C.F. C of E
8th Div.

Place	Date	Hour	Summary of Events and Information	Remarks and references to Appendices
ALBERT.	October 1916 19		S.C.F. visited 54th Field Ambulance Rest Station at VADENCOURT at which Rev. R.D. CANADINE is working. 54th Bde Chaplain Rev E.A. BENNET arrived with his Brigade in ALBERT from BOUZINCOURT. Chaplain D. RANDELL returned with 10th Essex Reg. 53rd Bde from Support line to ALBERT.	27
	21st		REGINA TRENCH Map 57. D S.E. co-ords R.22.2.73 to R.R.c 59a taken by Essex 8th Norfolk Regiments of 53rd Brigade. Chaplain D. RANDELL with M.O. of 10th Essex before, during, and after the action.	
	22nd		Sunday. Chaplains of 54th & 55th Brigades + Chaplain C.F. PARKINSON of 53rd Brigade cooperated with Senior Chaplain in holding largely attended voluntary services	

Army Form C. 2118

Vol III 67

WAR DIARY or S.C.L. C of E INTELLIGENCE SUMMARY 18th Div.

(Erase heading not required.)

28

Place	Date Hour	Summary of Events and Information	Remarks and references to Appendices
ALBERT	October 22nd 1916 (cont)	at Cinema Hall. RUE DES PRAIRIES, ALBERT. for all units of Division in or near the town, open also to officers & men from other Divisions. Early Celebrations of Holy Communion at 8.0 & 9.0 in S.C.A. room Abbots Row. Courts well attended — also 68 Communicants after morning service in Cinema Hall (a.t. 11.15 A.M.)	
"	25.	Rev. J.S. SHARP rejoined No. 2 Section 18th F.A.C. having left England after 10 days special leave Oct 21st inclusive occupied in travelling. Rev. R.D. CANADINE arrived with 54th Field Ambulance at BRICKFIELDS, ALBERT from VADENCOURT. Reports having had daily services whilst at REST	

Army Form C. 2118

Vol III 6.8.

WAR DIARY
or
S.C.F. INTELLIGENCE SUMMARY
18th Div
(Erase heading not required.)

29.

Place	Date	Hour	Summary of Events and Information	Remarks and references to Appendices
ALBERT	October 1916 25 (cont.)		Station, VADENCOURT. viz: Holy Communion in early morning & Service also Evening — with all well attended & apparently much appreciated.	
"	28th		Chaplain. R.D. CANADINE transferred from 54th Field Ambulance rejoined 8th R.f. Sussex Pioneers.	
"	29th		Services as last Sunday in Cinema Hall, ALBERT. Rev. R.D. CANADINE preaching in morning & Rev. V.C. Baddington in Evening — S.C.F. assisting.	

Oct 31st 1916. S.C.F.

G.A. Weston
C. of E.
18th Division

War Diary
of
the Senior Chaplain C. of E.
18th Division
for the month of
November 1916.

Volume IV.

S.C.F. C of E.
Vol. IV. p.1.
18th Div.

WAR DIARY
INTELLIGENCE SUMMARY

Place	Date Hour	Summary of Events and Information	Remarks and references to Appendices
ALBERT.	November 1916. 1.	Division holding REGINA TRENCH. Map 57D. S.E. R.22 a.7.3 to R.18.C.5.4 as since 21st October. Chaplain C.H. WELLER (atta. 12th Middlesex Reg't) left ENGLAND from leave after wound received at THIEPVAL (invalided from France Oct. 30th)	31
"	3	Senior Chaplain with Rev. R.D. CANADINE met IInd Corps C. of E. Chaplain Rev KINNEAR & Senior Chaplain 4th Canadian Division Rev GORDON at 4th Canadian Division's Free Coffee Stall, Tramway Crossing POZIERES ROAD. Map 57D. S.E. X.9.b.8.8. with a view to 2nd Corps assisted by 18th Division taking over this stall to allow Canadian Division to open stalls further forward. Corps Chaplain agreed to take over as soon as possible supplying stores, material & staff. S.C.F. C of E. + Rev. R.D. CANADINE obtaining local assistance commenced erecting new stall further back from Main Road	

Army Form C. 2118

WAR DIARY
or
INTELLIGENCE SUMMARY

S C F C of E
8th Div.

Vol IV. p.2.

32

Place	Date	Hour	Summary of Events and Information	Remarks and references to Appendices
ALBERT	November 1916 3	(cont'd)	2 Battalions of 55th & 2 battalions of 54th Bde relieved 53rd Brigade in the trenches. Chaplains N.C. BODDINGTON going up to the line with 7th Buffs.	
			Chaplain R.D. CANADINE superintending erection of new Coffee Stall started yesterday. Canadian Staff & supplies moved into & carried on serving of Coffee in new stall in afternoon.	
"	4		Chaplains D. RANDELL & C.T. PARKINSON moved back to WARLOY BAILLON with their Regiments which came out of line yesterday.	
			Chaplain E.A. BENNET returned from WARLOY BAILLON with 6th Northants. & Rev. C.H. WELLER returned to Division having left ENGLAND Nov. 1st after leave. Subsequent to G.S.W. in right arm.	

WAR DIARY
INTELLIGENCE SUMMARY

S.C.F. C of E. 18th Div.

Vol IV. p 3.

Army Form C. 2118

Place	Date	Hour	Summary of Events and Information	Remarks and references to Appendices
ALBERT	November 1916 5.		Joint Services for all units in Division in & near ALBERT held as on 2 previous Sundays — Celebrations of Holy Communion in Room opposite Law Courts, in RUE GRENIER À SEL at 7.0 AM, 8.0 AM & 9.0 AM. In Cinema Hall (RUE DES TRAIRIES) Morning Service at 10.30 AM followed by Holy Communion at 11.15 (76 Communicants) & Evening Service at 6.30 PM. Preacher in Morning, S.C.F. C of E. 18 Div. in Evening Rev. BAINES READ of 4th Canadian Division which is holding line on 18 Div right.	33
	6		Chaplain J.S. SHARP from 18th D.A.C. near MILLENCOURT came for 24 hours duty to 56 Field Ambulance M.D.S. ALBERT.	

WAR DIARY or INTELLIGENCE SUMMARY

Army Form C. 2118

P.C.I. CofE
Vol IV p 4.
18th Div.

Place	Date	Hour	Summary of Events and Information	Remarks and references to Appendices
ALBERT	Nov 6th 1916 (cont.)		Divisional ROUTINE ORDERS dated Nov. 5th publishing Decorations for Gallantry, included in list of those awarded the Military Cross Rev. E.A. BENNET. attached 6th Northants and Rev. C.H. WELLER " 12th Middlesex Regt. both of 54th Inf. Brigade. Above Chaplains went to trenches with their Battalions in afternoon – relieving other 2 battalions of 54th Inf. Brigade.	34
"	8th		S.C.F. II nd Corps took over running of Coffee Stall mentioned above under dates Nov 3 & 4 with Assistance of S.C.F. 18 Div. Rev. R.D. CANADINE, 18th Div. Salvage Coy. by instructions S.O. Branch H.Q. 18 Div. Supplying 4 men N.C.O. Supplies	

Place	Date Hour	Summary of Events and Information	Remarks and references to Appendices
ALBERT	Nov 1916 9th cont.	being sent from 2nd Corps (i.e. Coffee, Milk, Sugar, Stove &c) 53rd Brigade relieving Bns of 54th and 55th Brigades — Rev E.A. BENNETT (6th Northants) returned with their Battalion from trenches. Rev D. Randolphson (7th Buffs) Rev D. RANDELL (returned from WARLOY BAILLON yesterday) went up with 10th Essex Regt.	
	10th	Chaplain C.T. PARKINSON (attached 6th Royal Berks) 53rd Inf. Brigade left railhead on 10 days special leave — urgent family affairs. Chaplains BENNET & WELLER went to WARLOY BAILLON with their Battalions. Services held in Cinema Hall Albert for the 2 battalions of 54th & 55th Brigades in the town, by S.C.F. & Rev G.J. STOPFORD in conjunction with Chaplains of 1st Division for theirs & 5th Canadian troops.	35
"	11th 12th		

WAR DIARY or INTELLIGENCE SUMMARY

Army Form C. 2118

S.C.F. Co/E Vol IV p 6.
18th Divn

36

Place	Date Hour	Summary of Events and Information	Remarks and references to Appendices
ALBERT.	November 12th cont	S.C.F. also visited G.R.C. (HQ of Unit No 3) at WARLOY BAILLON & consulted Rev E.A. BENNET on matters connected with clearing of battlefields — marking of Graves under difficulties &c; a draft of instructions being under preparation by H.Q. of 18th Division.	
"	13th	S.C.F. visited A.C.G. V[th] Army re question of relief of Chaplains of 18th Division by incoming Division, when A Corps burying party continued to operate in an area after the Division which has been fighting was relieved. A.C.G. V[th] promised to write to S.C.F.s Corps & Divisions on the subject. Rev. E. A. BENNET. returned from WARLOY with 6th Northants to ALBERT. " C. H. WELLER " " Went to trenches to run free Soup Kitchen at R.23.C.10.4 Map 57.D. S.E. for men of 54th Bde in trenches.	

Army Form C. 2118

WAR DIARY
or
INTELLIGENCE SUMMARY

S.C.F. C. of E. 6th Div.

Vol IV. 67.

37

Place	Date	Hour	Summary of Events and Information	Remarks and references to Appendices
ALBERT.	November 1916 14		Chaplain V.C. BODDINGTON attached 7th Buffs 55th L.F.B9. transferred to 35th Casualty Clearing Station by orders through usual channel from A.C.G. IInd Army after report by S.C.F. in consultation with M.O. 7th Buffs that Rev. V.C. BODDINGTON having asthma was unfit for further work with the troops in and out of trenches in winter. Rev E.A. BENNET went up with his battalion to OVILLERS (huts) Rev. J.S. SHARP at Main Dressing Station — Rev R.D. CANADINE superintending Coffee Stall, Pozieres Road. S.C.F. received instructions from A.C.G. IInd Army that as general rule Chaplains should not be left behind	

WAR DIARY
or
INTELLIGENCE SUMMARY

Army Form C. 2118

S.C.7. C of I
18th Div.
Vol IV. p. 8.

Place	Date Hour November 1916	Summary of Events and Information	Remarks and references to Appendices
ALBERT	14 (cont)	Division with burial parties, when Division left an area, but should be relieved by Chaplains of incoming Division (unless party left behind were Divisional.) Letter dated yesterday.	32
"	16	54th Brigade came out of line to VILLERS Huts with Revs C. Weller & E.A. Bennet.	
	17. 7.30 & 9.0 AM	"V" "13.3" Shells dropped into Albert by enemy.	
	18th	55th Brigade attacked Hooky DESIRE TRENCH. Revd G.F. STOPFORD whilst taking German prisoners to Brig. was wounded slightly wounded in leg & returned with piece of shell — and returned to Q.M. 9 9th R.W. Kent Regt at Albert.	

Army Form C. 2118

WAR DIARY
or
INTELLIGENCE SUMMARY

S.C.F. C.E. Vol IV p.9
1st Div.

(Erase heading not required.)

Place	Date Hour	Summary of Events and Information	Remarks and references to Appendices
ALBERT	November 1916 19	Sunday. Larger attended Voluntary Services in Cinema Hall ALBERT taken by Rev. C.H. WELLER in Cooperation with Chaplain of 11th Canadian Div. S.C.F. & Rev. R.D. CANADINE at Main Dressing Station ALBERT. — Rev. D. RANDELL to WARLOY with his Battalion. Rev. G.F. STOPFORD temporarily transferred to Div. Rest Station VADENCOURT for light duty whilst recovering from slight leg wound received yesterday.	39
	8 P.M.	S.C.F. Visited Rev. Crick S.C.F. C.of E. 61st Div. at Contay re sending of relief for Rob's Free Coffee Stall, Pozieres Road, CONTAY & in particular re sending of relief for	
"	20	Rev. C.T. PARKINSON left England on his return from 10 days Special leave.	

WAR DIARY

S.C.F. C of E 18th Div. Vol IV f. 10.

Place	Date	Hour	Summary of Events and Information	Remarks
ALBERT	Nov 1916 21		Revs C.H. WELLER & E.A. BENNET started back for Rest area with their Brigade (54th)	40
	22.		Rev. R.D. CANADINE completed hand over of Corps Hee Coffee Stall. Began POZIÈRES ROAD (X.g.a8.8) to Rev. WINTER 61d Division & started back for rest area - temporarily attached 7th Buffs vice Rev. V.C. BODDINGTON previously transferred to C.C.S. Rev. G.F. STOPFORD relieves 7th R.W. Kents from 54th to 53rd Ambulance. S.C.F. C of E. left ALBERT to go (on horseback) to view D.H.Q in rest area, nr AMNS. Slept night at Candas CANDAS.	

Army Form C. 2118

WAR DIARY
or
S.C.F. C.of E. INTELLIGENCE SUMMARY 18th Div.

Vol IV. p11.

(Erase heading not required.)

Instructions regarding War Diaries and Intelligence Summaries are contained in F.S. Regs., Part II. and the Staff Manual respectively. Title Pages will be prepared in manuscript.

Place	Date	Hour	Summary of Events and Information	Remarks and references to Appendices
BUIGNY St MACLOU	November 1916 23rd		S.C.F. C.of E. arrived at Divisional Head Quarters, BUIGNY St MACLOU from ALBERT via CANDAS.	
	Sunday 25th		All Brigades still en route — S.C.F. held services for Divisional Head Qrs. at Village School BUIGNY	
"	28th		S.C.F. visited 5th Army Artillery School SAILLY LE SEC & referred to A.C.G. III Army in regard to appoint of Chaplain to 5th A. Artillery School	
"	30th		Chaplains Meeting of S.C.F.s billeted at BUIGNY at 11.30 AM — arrangements made to cover services for all units in area on following Sunday.	41 END

G.A. Weston
S.C.F. C.of E. 18th Division

Nov 30th 1916

www.ingramcontent.com/pod-product-compliance
Lightning Source LLC
Chambersburg PA
CBHW081457160426
43193CB00013B/2511